To:

_____

From:

_____

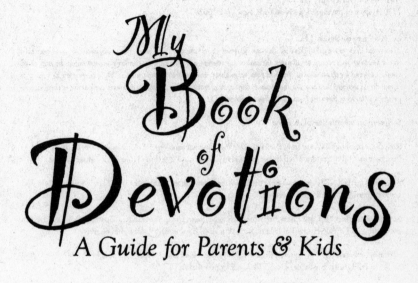

My Book of Devotions

A Guide for Parents & Kids

about Attitude

Simon & Schuster, Inc.

NEW YORK LONDON TORONTO SYDNEY

Simon & Schuster, Inc.

1230 Avenue of the Americas, New York, New York 10020

Cover Design by Kim Russell / Wahoo Designs
Page Layout by Bart Dawson

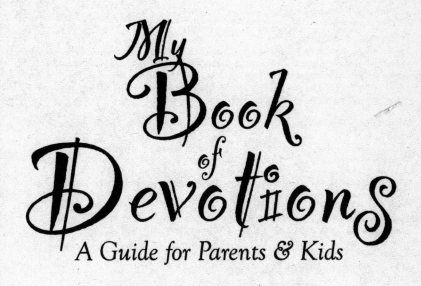

My Book of Devotions

A Guide for Parents & Kids

about Attitude

The Lord bless you and keep you;
The Lord make His face shine upon you,
And be gracious to you.

Numbers 6:24-25 NKJV

Table of Contents

A Message to Parents

Perhaps your child's bookshelf is already filled with a happy and helpful assortment of good books for kids. If so, congratulations—that means you're a thoughtful parent who understands the importance of reading to your child. This book is intended to be an important addition to your child's library.

This little text is intended to be read by Christian parents to their young children. The book contains 31 brief chapters, one for each day of the month. Each chapter consists of a Bible verse, a brief story, kid-friendly quotations from notable Christian thinkers, a timely tip, and a prayer. Every chapter examines a different aspect of an important topic: attitude.

For the next 31 days, take the time to read one chapter each night to your child, and then spend a few moments talking about the chapter's meaning. By the end of the month, you will have had 31 different opportunities to share God's wisdom with your son or daughter, and that's good . . . very good.

If you have been touched by God's love and His grace, then you know the joy that He has brought into your own life. Now it's your turn to share His message with the boy or girl whom He has entrusted to your care. Happy reading. And may God richly bless you and yours.

The Right Attitude

Your attitude should be the same
that Christ Jesus had.

Philippians 2:5 NLT

Day 1

What's an attitude? The word "attitude" means "the way that you think." And don't forget this: your attitude is important.

Your attitude can make you happy or sad, grumpy or glad, joyful or mad. And, your attitude doesn't just control the way that you think; it also controls how you behave. If you have a good attitude, you'll behave well. And if you have a bad attitude, you're more likely to misbehave.

Have you spent any time thinking about the way that you think? Do you pay much attention to your attitude? Hopefully so! After all, a good attitude is better than a bad one . . . lots better.

You have more control over your attitude than you think. So do your best to make your attitude a good attitude. One way you can do that is by learning about Jesus and about His attitude toward life. When you do, you'll learn that it's always better to think good thoughts, and it's always better to do good things. Always!

Big Idea for Kids

Learn about Jesus and His attitude. Then try to do what Jesus would do.

> Developing a positive attitude means working continually to find what is uplifting and encouraging.
> Barbara Johnson

Big Idea for Parents

Kids are amazingly intuitive: Believe it or not, your child is probably a mind reader. If your kid is like most kids, he or she is surprisingly sensitive. So do yourself and your child a favor: be careful with your thoughts as well as with your actions.

Today's Prayer

Dear Lord, I pray for an attitude
that pleases You. Even when I'm angry,
unhappy, tired, or upset, I pray that
I can remember what it means to be
a good person and a good Christian.

Amen

The Golden Rule

Dear friends, since God loved us that much,
we surely ought to love each other.
1 John 4:11 NLT

Day 2

Would you like to do something good today? If so, you can do it, and here's how: by obeying the Golden Rule.

Jesus told us that we should treat other people in the same way that we would want to be treated (that, of course, is the Golden Rule). But sometimes, especially when we're tired or upset, that rule is very hard to follow.

Jesus wants us to treat other people with respect, kindness, courtesy, and love. When we do, we make our families and friends happy . . . and we make our Father in heaven very proud.

So if you're wondering how to make the world a better place, here's a great place to start: let the Golden Rule be your rule, too. And if you want to know how to treat other people, ask the person you see every time you look into the mirror. The answer you receive will tell you exactly what to do.

Big Idea for Kids

Since you love them, say so! Since you sincerely love your family, make sure that you tell them so . . . a lot!

Be enthusiastic. Every occasion is
an opportunity to do good.
Russell Conwell

Big Idea for Parents

Jesus loves you, this you know . . . and your children should know this, too! Of course you know that Jesus loves you. But it's up to you to make sure that they know that you know. So remind them often.

Today's Prayer

Dear Lord, Your love is so wonderful
that I can't really imagine it,
but I can share it . . . and I will . . .
today and every day.
Amen

An Attitude of Joy

Light shines on those who do right;
joy belongs to those who are honest.
Rejoice in the Lord, you who do right.
Praise his holy name.

Psalm 97:11-12 NCV

Day 3

*G*od wants you to have a happy, joyful life. But that doesn't mean that you'll be happy all the time. Sometimes, you won't feel like feeling happy, and when you don't, your attitude won't be very good.

When you're feeling a little tired or sad, here's something to remember: This day is a gift from God. And it's up to you to enjoy this day by trying to be cheerful, helpful, courteous, and well behaved. How can you do these things? A good place to start is by doing your best to think good thoughts.

Big Idea for Kids

Sometimes happy, sometimes sad: Even if you're a very good person, you won't be happy all the time. Sometimes, things will happen to make you sad, and it's okay to be sad when bad things happen to you, to your friends, or to your family. But remember: through good times and bad, God is always with you, and you are always protected.

Jesus did not promise to change
the circumstances around us.
He promised great peace and pure joy
to those who would learn to believe that
God actually controls all things.
Corrie ten Boom

Big Idea for Parents

If you want to teach your child what it means to be a joyful Christian . . . be one.

Today's Prayer

Dear Lord, You have given me
so many blessings, starting with
my family. I will keep joy in my heart
as I thank You, Lord, for every single
blessing You've given me.
Amen

Self-control

So prepare your minds for service and have
self-control. All your hope should be for
the gift of grace that will be yours
when Jesus Christ is shown to you.

1 Peter 1:13 NCV

Day 4

Maybe you've heard this old saying: "Look before you leap." What does that saying mean? It means that you should stop and think before you do something. Otherwise you might be sorry you did it.

Learning how to control yourself is an important part of growing up. The more you learn about self-control, the better. Self-control will help you at home, at school, and at church. That's why parents and teachers are happy to talk about the rewards of good self-control. And that's why you should be excited about learning how important it is to look before you leap . . . not after!

Big Idea for Kids

Think first! Think before you say things . . . and think before you do things. Otherwise, you can get yourself in trouble. So here's a good rule to follow: Slow down long enough to think about the things you're about to do or say. That way, you'll make better choices.

Your thoughts are the determining factor
as to whose mold you are conformed to.
Control your thoughts and you control
the direction of your life.
Charles Stanley

Big Idea for Parents

Be an Example of Self-control: When it comes to parenting, you can't really teach it if you won't really live it.

Today's Prayer

Dear God, today I will slow down
and think about things before
I do them. And when I slow down
to think about things, I will always
try to do what's right.
Amen

Let's Be Thankful!

It is good to give thanks to the Lord,
to sing praises to the Most High.
It is good to proclaim your unfailing love
in the morning, your faithfulness
in the evening.
Psalm 92:1-2 NLT

Day 5

Do you have a thankful attitude? Hopefully so! After all, you've got plenty of things to be thankful for. Even during those times when you're angry or tired, you're a very lucky person.

Who has given you all the blessings you enjoy? Your parents are responsible, of course. But all of your blessings really start with God. That's why you should say "Thank You" to God many times each day. He's given you so much . . . so thank Him, starting now.

Big Idea for Kids

Two magic words: Thank you! Your parents will never get tired of hearing those two little words, and neither will your friends. And neither, for that matter, will God.

Thanksgiving is good
but Thanksliving is better.

Jim Gallery

Big Idea for Parents

You can't count all your blessings . . . there are simply too many of them. But, as a Christian parent, you know where to start counting: Your Heavenly Father, His only Son, and your own children.

Today's Prayer

Dear Lord, You have given me
so many blessings, and You want to give
me even more. Thank You. Here's how
I will show my thanks: I will have
a good attitude, I will be kind to
other people, and I will behave myself.

Amen

An Attitude That Makes God Happy

Therefore, whether we are at home or away,
we make it our aim to be pleasing to Him.
2 Corinthians 5:9 Holman CSB

Day 6

G od knows everything about you, including your attitude. And when your attitude is good, God is pleased . . . very pleased.

Are you interested in pleasing God? Are you interested in pleasing your parents? Your teachers? And you friends? If so, try to make your attitude the best it can be. When you try hard to have a good attitude, you'll make other people feel better—and you'll make yourself feel better, too.

Big Idea for Kids

How can you please God? By having a good attitude, by being obedient your parents and your teachers, and being kind to your friends.

If you try to please God and God alone, you'll find yourself satisfied with life.

Kay Arthur

Big Idea for Parents

The importance of a parent's attitude: Parental attitudes are contagious. It's up to you to live your life—and treat your family—in a way that pleases God because He's watching carefully . . . and so, for that matter, are your kids.

Today's Prayer

Dear Lord, thank You for all
the blessings You have given me.
Today and every day I will do my best
to please You by thinking good thoughts
and doing good deeds.
Amen

Respecting Other People

Show respect for all people.
Love the brothers and sisters of
God's family.
1 Peter 2:17 ICB

Day 7

Do you try to have a respectful attitude towards everybody? Hopefully so!

Should you be respectful of grown-ups? Of course. Teachers? Certainly. Family members? Yes. Friends? Yep, but it doesn't stop there. The Bible teaches us to treat all people with respect.

Respect for others is habit-forming: the more you do it, the easier it becomes. So start practicing right now. Say lots of kind words and do lots of kind things, because when it comes to kindness and respect, practice makes perfect.

Big Idea for Kids

Everybody is a VIP: VIP means "Very Important Person." To God, everybody is a VIP, and you should treat every person with dignity, patience, and respect.

If you will honor a person out of respect
for God, you can be assured that
God will honor you.

Beth Moore

Big Idea for Parents

Respect for all people: Children may seek to find humor in the misfortunes of others; children may, on occasion, exhibit cruelty towards other children. Be watchful for such behaviors and correct them with enthusiasm and vigor.

Today's Prayer

Dear Lord, let me remember to be
respectful and kind to everybody,
starting with my family and friends.
And, let me share the love that
I feel in my heart with them . . .
and with You!
Amen

When You Don't Feel Like Feeling Good

We must not become tired of doing good.
We will receive our harvest of eternal life at
the right time. We must not give up!

Galatians 6:9 ICB

Day 8

Where does a good attitude begin? It starts in our hearts and works its way out from there. Jesus taught us that a pure heart is a wonderful blessing. It's up to each of us to fill our hearts with love for God, love for Jesus, and love for all people. When we do, good things happen.

Sometimes, of course, we don't feel much like feeling good. Sometimes, when we're tired, or frustrated, or angry, we simply don't want to have a good attitude. On those days when we're feeling bad, it's time to calm down . . . and rest up.

Do you want to be the best person you can be? Then you shouldn't grow tired of doing the right things . . . and you shouldn't ever grow tired of thinking the right thoughts.

Big Idea for Kids

Want to feel better? Here are some things you can do: 1. Try not to misbehave. 2. Try to think good thoughts. 3. Try to cheer yourself up by cheering other people up. 4. Don't stay up late at night. And remember: if you're feeling really sick or really sad, tell your parents!

If you want to be truly happy,
be generous and kind.
Bill Hybels

Big Idea for Parents

Not feeling up to par? Try getting more sleep: If you're like most parents, you'll be tempted to get by on less sleep than you need. Don't do it. Make sure that you and your child go to bed early enough to get the sleep you need to feel good.

Today's Prayer

Dear Lord, when I am feeling
tired or sad, I can always talk to You,
and I can always talk to my parents, too.
Thanks for listening, Lord—
and thank You for parents who
are willing to listen and willing to help.
Amen

It Starts in the Heart

God has chosen you . . . . He loves you.
So always do these things: Show mercy to
others, be kind, humble, gentle, and patient.
Colossians 3:12 NCV

Day 9

An attitude of kindness starts in your heart and works its way out from there.

Do you listen to your heart when it tells you to be kind to other people? Hopefully, you do. After all, lots of people in the world aren't as fortunate as you are—and some of these folks are living very near you.

Ask your parents to help you find ways to do nice things for other people. And don't forget that everybody needs love, kindness, and respect, so you should always be ready to share those things, too.

Big Idea for Kids

Keep your eyes open for somebody to help: Someone very near you may need a helping hand or a kind word, so keep your eyes open, and look for people who need your help, whether at home, at church, or at school.

Without kindness, there can be no true joy.
Thomas Carlyle

Big Idea for Parents

It's good to feel compassion for others . . . but it's better to do something to ease their suffering. Martin Luther wrote, " Faith never asks whether good works are to be done, but has done them before there is time to ask the question, and it is always doing them." So when in doubt, do something good for somebody. That's how you'll teach your child the art and the joys of compassionate Christianity.

Today's Prayer

Dear Lord, let me help others in every way that I can. Jesus served others; I can, too. I will serve other people with my good deeds and with my prayers. And I will give thanks for everybody who helps me.

Amen

Watch What You Think

Fix your thoughts on what is true and honorable and right. Think about things that are pure and lovely and admirable. Think about things that are excellent and worthy of praise.

Philippians 4:8 NLT

Do you try to think the kind of thoughts that make you happy, not sad? The Bible says that you should.

Do you try to think about things that are true and right? The Bible says that you should.

Do you turn away from bad thoughts—and away from people who misbehave? The Bible says that you should.

The Bible instructs you to guard your thoughts against things that are hurtful or wrong. So remember this: when you turn away from the bad thoughts and bad people, you've made a very wise choice.

Big Idea for Kids

Good thoughts create good deeds. Good thoughts lead to good deeds, and bad thoughts lead elsewhere. So guard your thoughts accordingly.

The things we think are the things that feed our souls. If we think on pure and lovely things, we shall grow pure and lovely like them; and the opposite is also true.

Hannah Whitall Smith

Big Idea for Parents

Be positive: If your thoughts tend toward the negative end of the spectrum, redirect them. How? You can start by counting your blessings and by thanking your Father in heaven. And while you're at it, train yourself to begin thinking thoughts that are more rational, more accepting, and more upbeat (Philippians 4:8) . . . for your children's sake.

Today's Prayer

Dear Lord, help me think about things
that are good, things that are true,
and things that are right . . .
starting right now!
Amen

Words Are Important

Pleasant words are like a honeycomb.
They make a person happy and healthy.
Proverbs 16:24 ICB

Day 11

Do you like for people to say nice words to you? Yes, you do! And that's exactly how other people feel, too. That's why it's important to say things that make people feel better, not worse.

Your words can make other people feel better . . . or not. Make certain that you're the kind of person who says helpful things, not hurtful things. And, make sure that you're the kind of person who helps other people feel good about themselves.

Remember: everybody needs to hear kind words, and that's exactly the kind of words they should hear from you!

Big Idea for Kids

If you can't think of a nice thing to say . . .
please keep quiet. It's better to say nothing
than to hurt someone's feelings.

A lot of people have gone further than
they thought they could because
someone else thought they could.
Zig Ziglar

Big Idea for Parents

Words matter. The words you speak will help
shape the kids you love . . . and once you speak
those words, you cannot "un-speak" them. Even
if you're not speaking directly to your kids,
you can be sure that your kids are listening,
so choose your words carefully.

Today's Prayer

Dear Lord, I want the things that
I say to be pleasing to You.
Help me remember to be a kind person,
and help me say things that make
the world—and my heart—
a better place.
Amen

Let's Celebrate!

Rejoice in the Lord always.
I will say it again: Rejoice!
Philippians 4:4 Holman CSB

Day 12

Do you feel like celebrating today? Hopefully, you do feel like celebrating! After all, today (like every other day) should be a special time to thank God for all the wonderful things He has given you.

So don't wait for birthdays or holidays—make every day a special day, including this one. Take time to pause and thank God for His gifts. And then demonstrate your thanks by celebrating His world, His blessings, and His love.

Big Idea for Kids

Cheer up somebody else. Do you need a little cheering up? If so, find somebody else who needs cheering up, too. Then, do your best to brighten that person's day. When you do, you'll discover that cheering up other people is a wonderful way to cheer yourself up, too!

God is good, and heaven is forever.
Those two facts should brighten up
even the darkest day.
Marie T. Freeman

Big Idea for Parents

Cheerfulness is an attitude that is highly contagious: kids often catch it from their parents. Remember that cheerfulness starts at the top. A cheerful household usually begins with cheerful adults.

Today's Prayer

Dear Lord, You have given me so many reasons to be happy, and I want to be a cheerful Christian. Today and every day, I will do my best to share my happiness with my family and my friends.

Amen

Telling the Truth

The honest person will live safely,
but the one who is dishonest will be caught.

Proverbs 10:9 ICB

Day 13

What is your attitude about telling the truth? Should you be honest with your parents? Certainly. With your brothers and sisters? Of course. With cousins, grandparents, aunts and uncles? Yes! In fact, you should be honest with everybody in your family because honesty starts at home.

If you can't be honest in your own house, how can you expect to be honest in other places, like at church or at school? So make sure that you're completely honest with your family. If you are, then you're much more likely to be honest with everybody else.

Big Idea for Kids

It's better to say nothing: If you're tempted to say something that isn't true, don't say anything. A closed mouth tells no lies.

God doesn't expect you to be perfect,
but he does insist on complete honesty.
Rick Warren

Big Idea for Parents

Discuss the importance of honesty: Teach the importance of honesty every day, and, if necessary, use words.

Today's Prayer

Lord, sometimes it's hard to
tell the truth. But even when telling
the truth isn't easy, it's the right thing
to do. So, I'll do my best to tell
the truth—even when it's hard.
When I tell the truth, I'll be glad I did,
and my friends and parents
will be glad, too.
Amen

Choosing Friends Wisely

A friend loves you all the time.
Proverbs 17:17 ICB

Day 14

If your friends misbehave, do you misbehave right along with them, or do you tell them to stop? Usually, it's much easier to go along with your friends, even if you know they're misbehaving. But it's always better to do the right thing, even if it's hard.

Sometimes, grownups must stand up for the things they believe in. When they do, it can be hard for them, too. But the Bible tells us over and over again that we should do the right thing, not the easy thing.

When your friends misbehave, it can spoil everything. So if your friends behave badly, don't copy them! And if your friends keep behaving badly, choose different friends.

Big Idea for Kids

If you want to make new friends, how can you do it? A good way to make friends—and a good way to keep them—is to become a better listener. Most people are happy to tell you about themselves, and they'll be even happier if you listen carefully. So learn to be a good listener—it's a good way to make new friends.

Do you want to be wise? Choose wise friends.

Charles Swindoll

Big Idea for Parents

As parents, we can't make friendships for our children, but we can coach them on the art of making friends. All of us, whether youngsters or grown-ups, make friends by treating others as we wish to be treated. And if that sounds suspiciously like the Golden Rule, that's because it is the Golden Rule.

Today's Prayer

Dear Lord, other people may want
me to misbehave, but You want me to
behave myself. And that's what
I want, too—I want to do what's right.
So help me do the right thing, Lord,
even when it's hard.
Amen

Your Bible

Your word is like a lamp for my feet
and a light for my way.
Psalm 119:105 ICB

Day 15

The Bible is God's message to you, and He wants you to read it. If you and your parents read the Bible every day, you'll be reminded of God's rules, God's love, and God's Son Jesus.

Since the Bible is important to God, it should be important to you, too. In fact, the Bible is the most important book you'll ever own. It's God's Holy Word. Read it every day, and follow its instructions. If you do, you'll be glad you did . . . and so will God.

Big Idea for Kids

Try it, you'll like it! Give the Bible a try . . . the more you learn from it, the more you'll want to learn.

The surest, most productive,
and most effective way to receive
God's guidance is the Bible.
Bill Hybels

Big Idea for Parents

Children's Bible? Take a close look. If your child doesn't already own one, consider purchasing a translation of the Holy Bible specifically intended for children. These translations are amazingly helpful because of their simplicity and clarity.

Today's Prayer

Dear Lord, the Bible is Your gift to me.
Let me use it, let me trust it,
and let me obey it, today
and every day that I live.
Amen

No More Tantrums

Don't become angry quickly,
because getting angry is foolish.
Ecclesiastes 7:9 NCV

Day 16

Temper tantrums are so silly. And so is pouting. So, of course, is whining. When we lose our tempers, we say things that we shouldn't say, and we do things that we shouldn't do. Too bad!

The Bible tells us that it is foolish to become angry and that it is wise to remain calm. That's why we should learn to control our tempers before our tempers control us.

Big Idea for Kids

Time Out! If you become angry, the time to step away from the situation before you say unkind words or do unkind things—not after. It's perfectly okay to place yourself in "time out" until you can calm down.

Why lose your temper if, by doing so, you offend God, annoy other people, give yourself a bad time . . . and, in the end, have to find it again?

Josemaria Escriva

Big Idea for Parents

If you can control your anger, you'll help them see the wisdom in controlling theirs.

Today's Prayer

Dear Lord, help me to keep away
from angry thoughts and angry people.
And if I am tempted to have a temper
tantrum, help to calm down before I do.
Amen

When You Need to be Forgiven

Stop judging others, and you will not be
judged. Stop criticizing others,
or it will all come back on you.
If you forgive others, you will be forgiven.
Luke 6:37 NLT

Day 17

Do you ever make mistakes? Of course you do! Even if you're a very good person, you're bound to make a mistake or two—everybody does.

When you do something you shouldn't have done, here are some things you can do:

1. Apologize to the people you've hurt, and ask for their forgiveness;
2. Fix the things you've messed up or broken;
3. Don't make the same mistake again;
4. Ask God for His forgiveness (which, by the way, He will give to you instantly);
5. Get busy doing something you can be proud of;
6. Don't be too hard on yourself . . . even if you made a mistake, you're still a very, very special person!

Big Idea for Kids

Forgive other people . . . and keep forgiving! Sometimes, you may forgive somebody once and then, in a little while, you may become angry at the very same person again. If so, you must forgive that person again and again . . . until it sticks!

Jesus had a forgiving and understanding heart. If he lives within us,
mercy will temper our relationships
with our fellow men.
Billy Graham

Big Idea for Parents

Face facts: forgiveness can be a very hard thing to do. No matter. God instructs us to forgive others (and to keep forgiving them), period. As a parent, you must explain to your child that forgiving another person—even when it's difficult—is the right thing to do.

Today's Prayer

Dear Lord, I have made mistakes,
and You have forgiven me.
Thank You for Your forgiveness.
When I am not perfect,
help other people to forgive me—
and help me forgive myself.

Amen

You Can Do It...
If You Stick To It!

We must not become tired of doing good.
Galatians 6:2 ICB

Day 18

If you think you can do something, then you can probably do it. If you think you can't do something, then you probably won't do it.

So remember this: if you're having a little trouble getting something done, don't get mad, don't get frustrated, don't get discouraged, and don't give up. Just keep trying . . . and believe in yourself.

When you try hard—and keep trying hard— you can really do amazing things . . . but if you quit at the first sign of trouble, you'll miss out. So here's a good rule to follow: when you have something that you want to finish, finish it . . . and finish it sooner rather than later.

Big Idea for Kids

If things don't work out at first, don't quit. If you never try, you'll never know how good you can be.

Don't quit. For if you do,
you may miss the answer to your prayers.
Max Lucado

Big Idea for Parents

Remember the advice of Winston Churchill: He said, "Never give in; never give in; never give in." And that's good advice whether you're leading a nation or a family.

Today's Prayer

Dear Lord, when I want to give up,
help me remember how important it is
to keep trying. And when I'm worried
or upset, help me remember to talk
to my parents and to You.

Amen

Don't Be Too Hard on Yourself

If you hide your sins, you will not succeed.
If you confess and reject them,
you will receive mercy.

Proverbs 28:13 NCV

Day 19

When you make a mistake, do you get really mad at yourself . . . or maybe really, really, really mad? Hopefully not! After all, everybody makes mistakes, and nobody is expected to be perfect.

Even when you make mistakes, God loves you . . . so you should love yourself, too.

So the next time you make a mistake, learn from it. And after you've learned your lesson, try never to make that same mistake again. But don't be too hard on yourself. God doesn't expect you to be perfect, and since He loves you anyway, you should feel that way, too.

Big Idea for Kids

When you make a mistake, learn something . . . and forgive someone: yourself. Remember, you don't have to be perfect to be wonderful.

The happiest people in the world are not
those who have no problems,
but the people who have learned to live
with things that are less than perfect.

James Dobson

Big Idea for Parents

Parents aren't perfect either: The perfect parent does not exist. So don't be too hard on yourself when you fall short of absolute perfection (or, for that matter, when you fall short of near perfection). Do your best, and trust God with the rest.

Today's Prayer

Dear Lord, when I ask for
Your forgiveness, You give it.
When I make mistakes,
help me to learn my lessons . . .
and help me to forgive myself.
Amen

A Peaceful Heart, A Peaceful Home

I leave you peace; my peace I give you.
I do not give it to you as the world does.
So don't let your hearts be
troubled or afraid.

John 14:27 NCV

Day 20

Jesus offers us peace . . . peace in our hearts and peace in our homes. But He doesn't force us to enjoy His peace—we can either accept His peace or not.

When we accept the peace of Jesus Christ by opening up our hearts to Him, we feel much better about ourselves, our families, and our lives.

Would you like to feel a little better about yourself and a little better about your corner of the world? Then open up your heart to Jesus, because that's where real peace begins.

Big Idea for Kids

God's peace can be yours right now . . . if you open up your heart and invite Him in.

Peace with God is where all peace begins.
Jim Gallery

Big Idea for Parents

Peace at home . . . As the parent, you're in charge of keeping the peace and sharing it. It's a big job, so don't be afraid to ask for help . . . especially God's help.

Today's Prayer

Dear Lord, I will open my heart to You.
And I thank you, God, for Your love,
for Your peace, and for Your Son.
Amen

Count Your Blessings . . . and Keep Counting!

I pray also that you will have greater understanding in your heart so you will know the hope to which he has called us and that you will know how rich and glorious are the blessings God has promised his holy people.

Ephesians 1:18-19 NCV

Day 21

If you sat down and began counting your blessings, how long would it take? A very, very long time! Your blessings include your life, your family, your friends, your talents, and possessions, for starters. But, your greatest blessing—a gift that is yours for the asking—is God's gift of eternal life through Christ Jesus.

You can never count up every single blessing that God has given you, but it doesn't hurt to try . . . so get ready, get set, go—start counting your blessings RIGHT NOW!

Big Idea for Kids

Want to cheer yourself up? Count your blessings. If you need a little cheering up, start counting your blessings . . . and keep counting until you feel better.

Jesus intended for us to be overwhelmed by the blessings of regular days. He said it was the reason he had come: "I am come that they might have life, and that they might have it more abundantly."

Gloria Gaither

Big Idea for Parents

Be imaginative: There are so many ways to say, "I love you." Find them. Put love notes in lunch pails and on pillows; hug relentlessly; laugh, play, and pray with abandon. Remember that love is highly contagious, and that your task, as a parent, is to ensure that your children catch it.

Today's Prayer

Dear Lord, today I will begin counting
my blessings . . . and I will keep
counting them every day of my life.
Amen

Excuses, Excuses, Excuses...

You, therefore, have no excuse,
you who pass judgment on someone else,
for at whatever point you judge the other,
you are condemning yourself.
Romans 2:1 NIV

Day 22

What is an excuse? Well, when you make up an excuse, that means that you try to come up with a good reason that you didn't do something that you should have done.

Anybody can make up excuses, and you can too. But you shouldn't get into the habit of making too many excuses. Why? Because excuses don't work. And why don't they work? Because everybody has already heard so many excuses that almost everybody can recognize excuses when they hear them.

So the next time you're tempted to make up an excuse, don't. Instead of making an excuse, do what you think is right. After all, the very best excuse of all . . . is no excuse.

Big Idea for Kids

The habit of making excuses is a bad habit. Excuses lead to trouble. If you're in the habit of making excuses, the best day to stop that habit is today.

> Replace your excuses with
> fresh determination.
>
> Charles Swindoll

Big Idea for Parents

Excuses, excuses, excuses: As parents of young children, we hear lots and lots of excuses, some of which are valid, but many of which are not. It's our job to determine the difference between valid excuses and imaginary ones, and then to help our children understand the difference between the two.

Today's Prayer

Dear Lord, help me to do the right
thing when it needs to be done . . .
so that I won't need to make excuses.
Amen

Blaming Others . . .

An angry person causes trouble.
Proverbs 29:22 NCV

Day 23

When something goes wrong, do you look for somebody to blame? And do you try to blame other people even if you're the one who made the mistake? Hopefully not!

It's silly to try to blame other people for your own mistakes, so don't do it.

If you've done something you're ashamed of, don't look for somebody to blame; look for a way to say, "I'm sorry, and I won't make that same mistake again."

Big Idea for Kids

Blaming others is easy . . . but it's usually wrong. Fixing mistakes is harder . . . but it's usually right.

> You'll never win the blame game,
> so why even bother to play?
>
> Marie T. Freeman

Big Idea for Parents

Parents set the tone: It's easy (and quite natural) for your child to find fault in others and spread blame to others. That's why it's up to you, as parent, to teach your child to take responsibility . . . and to learn from his or her mistakes!

Today's Prayer

Dear Lord, when I make a mistake,
I want to admit it. Help me not blame
others for the mistakes that I make.
And when I make a mistake,
help me to learn from it.
Amen

Let's Laugh!

There is a time for everything, and
everything on earth has its special season.
There is a time to cry and a time to laugh.
There is a time to be sad and
a time to dance.
Ecclesiastes 3:1,4 NCV

Day 24

Do you like to laugh? Of course you do! Laughter is a gift from God that He hopes you'll use in the right way. So here are a few things to remember:

1. God wants you to be happy. 2. Laughter is a good thing when you're laughing at the right things. 3. You should laugh with people, but you should never laugh at them.

God created laughter for a reason...and God knows best. So do yourself a favor: laugh at the right things . . . and laugh a lot!

Big Idea for Kids

Laughter is good medicine: So here's your prescription: Laugh lots!

> If you want people to feel comfortable
> around you, to enjoy being with you,
> then learn to laugh at yourself and
> find humor in life's little mishaps.
>
> Dennis Swanberg

Big Idea for Parents

Are we having fun yet? As a parent, it's up to you to make certain that your house is a place where everybody can expect to have good clean fun and plenty of laughs. How can you do so? By making certain that the good clean fun begins with you. Remember: if you're not having fun, neither, in all likelihood, are your kids.

Today's Prayer

Dear Lord, laughter is Your gift.
Today and every day, put a smile on
my face, and let me share that
smile with my friends and family . . .
especially my family.
Amen

Looking for the Good Things

Summing it all up, friends, I'd say you'll do best by filling your minds and meditating on things true, noble, reputable, authentic, compelling, gracious, the best, not the worst.

Philippians 4:8 MSG

Day 25

If you look for the good in other people, you'll probably find it. And, if you look for the good things in life, you'll probably find them, too.

But if you spend your time looking for things that aren't so good, you'll most certainly find plenty of bad things to look at. So what should you do? It's simple: you should look for the good things, of course.

When you start looking for good things, you'll find them everywhere: in church, at school, in your neighborhood, and at home.

So don't waste your time on things that make you feel angry, discouraged, worried, guilty, or afraid. Look, instead, for the good things in life, the things that God wants you to pay attention to. You'll be glad you did . . . and God will be glad, too.

Big Idea for Kids

Before you watch anything on television . . . ask your parents if it's okay.

You can be sure you are abiding in Christ if you are able to have a Christlike love toward the people that irritate you the most.

Vonette Bright

Big Idea for Parents

What should you allow them to watch on TV? Before you decide which programs are appropriate for your child, ask yourself this question: Does God approve?

Today's Prayer

Dear Lord, Let my words and my deeds
be good. Let me praise You, Father,
by following in the footsteps of
Your Son, and let others see
Him through me.
Amen

What Solomon Said

You must choose for yourselves today
whom you will serve . . . as for me and
my family, we will serve the Lord.
Joshua 24:15 NCV

Day 26

Solomon was a king, a very wise man, and a very good writer. He even wrote several books in the Bible! So when He finally put down His pen, what was this wise man's final advice? It's simple: Solomon said: "Honor God and obey His commandments."

The next time you have an important choice to make, ask yourself this: "Am I honoring God and obeying Him? And am I doing what God wants me to do?" If you can answer those questions with a great big "YES," then go ahead. But if you're uncertain if the choice you are about to make is the right one, slow down. Why? Because that's what Solomon says . . . and that's what God says, too!

Big Idea for Kids

Wise choices bring you happiness; unwise choices don't. So whenever you have a choice to make, choose wisely.

Life is a series of choices between
the bad, the good, and the best.
Everything depends on how we choose.
Vance Havner

Big Idea for Parents

Some choices are up to the parents: Certainly, we want to give our children the chance to make decisions on their own, but some decisions must be reserved for the wisest men and women of the family (responsible parents like you). When it comes to the health, well-being, and safety of your child, you must decide.

Today's Prayer

Lord, help me to make choices that are pleasing to You. Help me to be honest, patient, and kind. And above all, help me to follow the teachings of Jesus, not just today, but every day.
Amen

A Happy Heart...
Day by Day

Create in me a pure heart, God,
and make my spirit right again.
Psalm 51:10 NCV

Day 27

If we could decide to be happy "once and for all," life would be so much simpler, but it doesn't seem to work that way. If we want happiness to last, we need to create good thoughts every day that we live. Yesterday's good thoughts don't count . . . we've got to think more good thoughts today.

Each new day is a gift from God, so treat it that way. Think about it like this: today is another wonderful chance to celebrate God's gifts.

So celebrate—starting now—and keep celebrating forever!

Big Idea for Kids

A happy heart every day: Remember: You can choose to have a good attitude or a not-so good attitude. And it's a choice you make every day.

If you want to be truly happy,
you won't find it on an endless quest
for more stuff. You'll find it in receiving
God's generosity and then passing
that generosity along.
Bill Hybels

Big Idea for Parents

A Positive Attitude is Contagious . . . your children can catch it from you . . . and they should!

Today's Prayer

Dear Lord, help me have an attitude
that is pleasing to You as I count
my blessings today, tomorrow,
and every day.
Amen

Looking at the Donut

You fill my cup to overflowing.
Surely your goodness and love will be
with me all my life, and I will live
in the house of the Lord forever.
Psalm 23:5-6 NCV

Day 28

Here's a poem that was seen many years ago in a small donut shop: "As you travel through life, brother, Whatever be your goal, Keep your eye upon the donut, And not upon the hole."

What do you think these words mean? Well, this little poem can teach you an important lesson: You should spend more time looking at the things you have, not worrying about the things you don't have.

When you think about it, you've got more blessings than you can count. So make it a habit to thank God for the gifts He's given you, and don't feel jealous, angry, or sad about all the other stuff.

Big Idea for Kids

Think about all the things you have (starting with your family and your faith) . . . and think about all the things you can do! If you think you can do something, you probably can. If you think you can't do something, you probably can't. That's why it's so important to believe in yourself.

> Optimism and cheerfulness are
> products of knowing Christ.
> Billy Graham

Big Idea for Parents

Avoid Cynicism, Spread Optimism: Cynicism is contagious, and so is optimism. Maya Angelou observed, "A cynical young person is almost the saddest sight to see, because it means that he or she has gone from knowing nothing to believing nothing." Raise your children accordingly.

Today's Prayer

Lord, I will look for the best in other people, I will expect the best from You, and I will try my best to do my best—today and every day.

Amen

Let's Praise God!

Great is the Lord!
He is most worthy of praise!

Psalm 145:3 NLT

Day 29

The Bible makes it clear: it pays to say "thank You" to God. But sometimes, we may not feel like thanking anybody, not even our Father in heaven.

If we ever stop praising God, it's a big mistake . . . a VERY BIG mistake.

When you stop to think about it, God has been very generous with you . . . and He deserves a great big "thanks" for all those amazing gifts.

Do you want an attitude that pleases God? Then make sure that your attitude praises God. And don't just praise Him on Sunday morning. Praise Him every day, starting with this one.

Big Idea for Kids

Praise Him! One of the reasons you go to church is to praise God. But, you need not wait until Sunday rolls around to thank your Heavenly Father. Instead, you can praise Him many times each day by saying silent prayers that only He can hear.

The time for praise is now.
Let us begin to do our part now.
Hannah Whitall Smith

Big Idea for Parents

Want to cheer yourself up? Count your blessings If you need a little cheering up, start counting your blessings . . . and keep counting until you feel better.

Today's Prayer

Dear Lord, today I will thank You for
all Your blessings. And I'll do the same
thing tomorrow, and every day after
that. You never stop loving me,
and I will never stop praising You.
Amen

The Decision to Do What's Right

The LORD has already told you
what is good, and this is what he requires:
to do what is right, to love mercy,
and to walk humbly with your God.

Micah 6:8 NLT

Day 30

In the Book of Proverbs, King Solomon gave us wonderful advice for living wisely. Solomon said that we should keep our eyes "focused on what is right." In other words, we should do our best to say and do the things that we know are pleasing to God.

The next time you're tempted to say an unkind word or to say something that isn't true, remember the advice of King Solomon. Solomon knew that it's always better to do the right thing, even when it's tempting to do otherwise. So if you know something is wrong, don't do it; instead, do what you know to be right. When you do, you'll be saving yourself a lot of trouble, and you'll be obeying the Word of God.

Big Idea for Kids

No so fast! If you're about to do something, but you're not sure if it's the right thing to do, slow down! It's better to make a good decision than a fast decision.

> If you lack knowledge, go to school.
> If you lack wisdom, pray about it.
> Vance Havner

Big Idea for Parents

Helping your child make wise choices . . . it's not just important to teach your child what to think. It's also important to teach your child how to think (and there's a big difference between the two).

Today's Prayer

Dear Lord, there's a right way to do
things and a wrong way. Help me to do
things the right way today
and every day.
Amen

Jesus Loves Me, This I Know

And I am convinced that nothing can ever separate us from his love. Whether we are high above the sky or in the deepest ocean, nothing in all creation will ever be able to separate us from the love of God that is revealed in Christ Jesus our Lord.

Romans 8:38–39 NLT

Day 31

Perhaps you've heard these words before: "Jesus loves me, this I know, for the Bible tells me so." Of course, these words can be found in the song "Jesus Loves Me." It's a wonderful song that should remind you of something very important: Jesus loves you very much.

When you invite Jesus to become your friend, He will do it . . . and He'll be your friend forever. If you make mistakes, He'll still be your friend. If you misbehave, He'll still love you. If you feel sorry or sad, He can help you feel better.

Yes, Jesus loves you more than you know. And when you welcome Him into your heart, you will be blessed now and forever.

Big Idea for Kids

What a friend you have in Jesus: Jesus loves you, and He offers you eternal life with Him in heaven. Invite Him into your heart. Now!

Live your lives in love, the same sort of love
which Christ gives us, and which
He perfectly expressed when He gave
Himself as a sacrifice to God.

Corrie ten Boom

Big Idea for Parents

Think about His blessings: Today, as you hug your child or kiss your spouse—or as you gaze upon a passing cloud or marvel at a glorious sunset—think of what God has done for you and yours. And, every time you notice a gift from the Giver of all things good, praise Him. His works are marvelous, His gifts are beyond understanding, and His love endures forever.

Today's Prayer

Dear Jesus, I know that You love me
today and that You will love me forever.
And I thank You for Your love . . .
today and forever.

Amen

Bible Verses
to Remember

For God so loved the world
that he gave his only Son,
so that everyone who believes in him
will not perish but have eternal life.

John 3:16 NLT

Anything is possible if a person believes.

Mark 9:23 NLT

But happy are those . . . whose hope is in the LORD their God.

Psalm 146:5 NLT

Be still,
and know that I am God . . . .

Psalm 46:10 KJV

Choose for yourselves this day
whom you will serve . . .
as for me and my household,
we will serve the LORD.

Joshua 24:15 NIV

My purpose is to give life in all its fullness.

John 10:10 Holman CSB

Ask and it will be given to you; seek and you will find.

Matthew 7:7 NIV

Are any among you suffering?
They should keep on praying about it.

James 5:13 NLT

A person who does not quickly get
angry shows that he has understanding.
But a person who quickly loses
his temper shows his foolishness.

Proverbs 14:29 ICB

Foolish people are always getting into quarrels, but avoiding quarrels will bring you honor.

Proverbs 20:3 ICB

And yet the reason
you don't have
what you want is that
you don't ask God for it.

James 4:2 NLT

Finally brothers, whatever is true,
whatever is honorable,
whatever is just, whatever is pure,
whatever is lovely, whatever is
commendable—if there is
any moral excellence and if there is
any praise—dwell on these things.

Philippians 4:8 Holman CSB

Be an example to
the believers in word,
in conduct, in love,
in spirit, in faith,
in purity.

1 Timothy 4:12 NKJV

All things are possible for the one who believes.

Mark 9:23 NCV

But grow in grace,
and in the knowledge of
our Lord and Saviour
Jesus Christ . . . .

2 Peter 3:18 KJV

He did it with all his heart, and prospered.

2 Chronicles 31:21 KJV

The Lord bless you
and keep you;
The Lord make His face
shine upon you,
And be gracious to you.

Numbers 6:24-25 NKJV